HOW I SURVIVED THE
IRISH FAMINE

THE JOURNAL OF MARY O'FLYNN

Laura Wilson

Gill & Macmillan

HOW I SURVIVED THE IRISH FAMINE

Published in Ireland by
Gill & Macmillan Ltd
Hume Avenue, Park West
Dublin 12
with associated companies throughout the world
www.gillmacmillan.ie
Volume © 2000 by Breslich & Foss Limited, London
0 7171 3150 5

Designed by Nigel Osborne
Print origination by Global Colour Separation
Printed by Artegrafica, Italy

Published by arrangement with
Breslich & Foss Limited, London

3 5 4 2

Acknowledgments
Breslich & Foss would like to thank Mary Heffernan, Michael
Rimmer, Emma Bergamin Davys, Marianne Bergamin Davys,
Mary Blake, Monica Winters and Richard Hurst at the Ulster
American Folk Park, Declan Jones and John O'Driscoll at the
Famine Museum, Strokestown Park.

Picture Credits
Bridgeman Art Library: pp26-27; Bridgeman/Watts Gallery;
p31(top right); Dept of Irish Folklore, University College
Dublin: pp10-11; Fine Art Photographic Library: pp28-29;
Hulton Getty: p12(top left), p15(bottom), pp22-23, pp24-25,
p29, p31(bottom); Illustrated London News: pp18-19;
Strokestown Park: pp16-17(background) The Poor House,
Co.Sligo - Michael McCarthy; Strokestown Park Famine
Museum: pp8-9, 10(top & bottom), 11, 16, 17, 18(right & bot-
tom), 22, 24; Ulster American Folk Park: pp8, 9, 10(center),
12(bottom), 13, 14(left), 15(top), 18(top), 19(background), 20,
23, 26, 27(top), 28-9.

All other photographs by Mike Slingsby. Images on pp2-3, 12-
13, 14-15, 22-23, 24, 32-33, 34-35 photographed in Galway.

Maps by Phil Richardson

Contents

Introduction 4
Mary's Journal 6

INTRODUCTION

The Irish potato famine of the 1840s was the last major famine in Europe. Although there had been famines in Ireland before — those of 1739–41, 1816–17, 1822 and 1831 killed thousands of people — the one that started in 1845 was the worst of all. By 1850, a million people had died of starvation or disease, and a further one and a half million had fled the country.

The direct cause of the famine was the "blight," a fungus called *phytophtora infestans* that destroys potato plants. During the summer of 1845, it had devastated potato harvests across Europe. Although the loss of the European crops resulted in hardship, the consequences were nowhere near as severe as they were in Ireland.

The loss of the Irish potato crop was a terrible disaster because many people had, quite literally, nothing else to eat. In the 1840s, one third of all arable land in Ireland was used to grow potatoes and these, together with a little buttermilk, were the staple food for most of the year. Although it might have been a very boring diet, it was not a particularly bad one —

travelers to Ireland at this time often remarked that, although the people were poor, they looked healthy. Potatoes are a high-yielding crop. Even with an adult man eating as many as 14 pounds in one day, a single acre of land could produce enough potatoes to feed six people for almost a year. The harvest usually lasted for about ten months. Potatoes were dug up in August, so June and July were often difficult months, with little to eat. Those who lived near the sea could eat fish, and in some parts of the country people ate oatmeal biscuits and porridge or "stirabout." Families who could afford it kept a pig and a few hens to add occasional meat and eggs to their diet.

In 1841, there were over eight million people living in Ireland. Around seven million of these lived in the country, as tenants of the Anglo-Irish families who owned the land at that time. Many of these landlords preferred to live in England. They either left the management of their vast estates to agents, or rented their land to rich farmers who were known as "middlemen." These, in turn, rented out smaller portions of land to poorer farmers, most of whom grew corn that they sold to pay the rent, and potatoes to feed their families. Most of these small farms were less than five acres, and the laborers were often paid for their work by being given a rough cabin to live in and a small plot of land for planting potatoes. Most landlords had the right to throw their tenants out of their houses at a moment's notice. This usually happened if the rent had not been paid, or if the landlord or middleman decided that he would prefer to use the land for grazing cattle or sheep.

All of this made Ireland, in 1845, a country where many people lived in conditions of poverty and insecurity, depending on the annual potato crop for survival. Unfortunately, the potato that was the most widely grown — the "lumper" or "horse potato" — was one of the least resistant to the blight.

Although some attempts were made by the British government to help the famine victims, most of the politicians of the time believed in the philosophy of "laissez faire." This meant that they preferred not to send aid, but to leave things to take their course. For millions of sufferers, the help that came was too little and too late. Although it is true that far more could, and should, have been done, very little was known at the time about how to give medical and economic help to famine victims. Even today — over 150 years later — when we have better understanding about aid programs for those in need, many people in the world face death from starvation every day.

In the years before the famine, the Irish language was widely spoken in Ireland, and it is not likely that a girl such as Mary O'Flynn would have been able to speak much English. It is also unlikely that she would have been able to keep a journal — education in Ireland was very limited at this time, and it is thought that only 30 percent of the population could read and write. Although "Mary O'Flynn" never existed, and specific details of the famine tend to vary from county to county — for example, suffering was generally greater in the west of Ireland than in the east — the ordeal of the O'Flynn family is broadly representative of the terrible suffering experienced by millions of Irish people during 1845–51.

Mary's Journal

While I am minding the little ones, I weave baskets to carry the turf from the fields. I am trying to teach my sister Margaret, but her hands are not yet strong enough to twist the wood.

I'd say you'll be wanting to know about my family first, so let me tell you. My father is Sean O'Flynn, and he has a farm. Not his own — if you meet an Irishman who says he is the owner of his land, then your man is telling you a tale, for it all belongs to the English. If I brought you to our house and you stood in the doorway and looked about you, every field that you would see belongs to Major Lloyd.

My mother's name is Mary, and that is my name, too. I am twelve years of age and the eldest of her six children. Michael is the best of my brothers; he is eleven years old and as bold as you like. Then comes Patrick, who is eight, and my sister Margaret. She's six years old. After that come Seamus, who is two, and baby Annie. My grandmother Ann

Tierney lives in our house with us. How old she is I cannot tell you, for nobody knows, not even herself.

My father's farm is of a good size: four acres. He grows corn to sell, and potatoes to feed ourselves and the animals — we keep a cow, a pig, and some fowls. I help my mother look after the house and mind the little ones, and Michael and Patrick help my father in the fields. My father has Pat Feeney to work for him besides. Pat lives with his wife and five children in a cabin, not far from here.

A Staple Diet

Twice a day I prepare the potatoes for our meals. They are covered in earth from the fields, and must be washed. I cannot imagine a world where there are no potatoes — what would there be for the poor people to eat?

APRIL 1845

Mother told me I'm to bring some buttermilk to Pat Feeney, so I filled up the large measuring cup — the noggin — and went away with it down the road to the cabin.

When I got there I found that Pat was helping my father to plant his seed potatoes, but Pat's wife, Bridget, called out to me to watch where I stepped, for she was teeming the spuds. It was a lucky thing I looked before I put my foot down, because there on the doorstep at my feet was a basket of cooked potatoes laid down for the water to drain off. The cabin being quite dark within but for a small fire, I was about to step right into the middle of the supper! Bridget brought the basket inside and set it down on the earthen floor. On the stool beside it, she placed some salt she had in a twist of paper. Then the children came, and gathered round, some sitting on stools and some on the floor — there being not so many stools as there are children in the Feeney cabin. The children passed the noggin between themselves, and, when each had a drink taken, they picked up their potatoes, dipped them in the salt, and began to eat.

Pat Feeney's small cabin is fierce drafty, for there is no glass in the window, but a piece of dried sheepskin.

A Supper of Potatoes

I went home to a grand supper, for mother was after making potato cakes to use up the boiled spuds left over from the dinner. When all the water is drained off, take each potato in your hand and peel it with your thumbnail. If you keep your nail at a good length, you'll soon have the soft peel off faster than if you'd used a knife. Put by the peel for your pig, then pound up the rest with milk and a pinch of salt. Break the mixture into pieces as well as you can, and bake it over the fire until it is ready. 'Tis pleasant to eat with a little butter and a drink of milk. Then, if you have some potatoes in the bottom of your pot that are not boiled through, put them down in the embers with red coals on top and leave them there till you eat them as an after course, with their burned skin.

Our house has thick walls made from stone, a thatched roof and floors of beaten earth. It has three good rooms. At the front, next to the path, there is a great heap of dung we use to spread upon the soil. Our landlord is Major Lloyd. I have never seen him but he stays in the big house whenever he visits Ireland.

JULY–AUGUST 1845

Our house being a noisy place with children and chickens always underfoot, it is nice to be by yourself for a while. This afternoon, as soon as my work was done, I walked out into the lane. The sun was bright and every field and garden was shining with potato plants, their stalks green and thick and strong. I closed my eyes for a moment, and then I heard Father come up behind me. I'd no time to run and I thought he would give out to me for wasting time, but he just looked around him and smiled. "Well, Mary," says he, "I'd say it'd be a grand crop this year, please God."

That was the last day of the good weather. After that, we'd rain and fog and gloom for three weeks, and two days ago a blue mist the like of which no one had ever seen before came in from the sea. It was so thick

Seed potatoes are laid on spade-dug beds and covered over with a ridge of soil. Between the ridges are drainage channels that are cut using a loy like this one (above). Potatoes are harvested in late August and stored in pits.

This year, all our neighbors' crops are ruined by the blight. The despair on their faces is terrible to see.

that you couldn't see your hand in front of your face, and when it cleared, all the stalks and leaves of the potato plants were black and hanging down as if they were dead. The stench of it was desperate. I brought my grandmother out of the house to smell the smell that was coming off the fields. She looked about her for a long time and then she shook her head and said, "This is the devil's own work."

I have heard many stories about the food they eat at the big house. I often think how much I should like to have a smell of the kitchen with the meat cooking and see the great table made ready for dinner, with more dishes set upon it than you could ever hope to count. Then I think of the ladies and gentlemen and the fine clothes on them and I wonder, would they ever look at a potato?

SEPTEMBER 1845

When my father saw what had happened in the potato fields, he called Michael to come away and help him dig the spuds and get them up out of the ground. I sat in the house and minded the little ones, and after a time my grandmother asked me to bring her again to the field. She shook her head as she had done before, and when I asked her why, she said, "I have not a notion what it might be, but it is not a good thing." Then she said that it must be God's judgment for the waste in other years, throwing good potatoes into the ditch because there were so many. Then she turned to go back to the house. I asked, "Will I not help you, grandmother?" but she said, "Away with you and help your brother."

I knelt down to pick up the potatoes that were dug out of the ground. They were small enough, to be sure, but I could see nothing bad about them. Soon my apron was covered with mud and I felt cold and damp all over, but I kept on working until it grew dark and it was time to go back to the house.

My father went with Pat Feeney to the bog to cut turf for the fire. The slane (far right) is what they use to cut the sods of turf and lift them away from the bank.

Cooking with Rotten Potatoes

My mother cooked some of the potatoes we brought from the field, and when they were drained we saw the dirt on them. My grandmother said, "You have set them to boil without washing," but Mother said no, she had cleaned the potatoes, but there was something about them that was not as it should be. When we broke them open, we saw that inside, some parts were good and some parts rotten. Grandmother told her not to set any more potatoes to boil, but to make boxty instead. So we grated the rest of the spuds to make a pulp which we pounded into round, flat cakes. These we laid on the red coals of the fire to cook — first on one side and then on the other. And that is how you make boxty, which is bread from raw potatoes.

Our kitchen has a settle bed by the fire. If you want to sleep in it, you may lift up the top and step inside. I share a bed with my sister Margaret, but once when she fell sick I had to sleep in the settle bed. It felt very strange to be all alone and quiet, with wooden walls set around my head, and many times I woke afraid, thinking myself to be in a coffin.

AUGUST 1846

I went to Pat's cabin. The children were crouched about the remains of the fire, and all looked weak and sick. When I asked for their mother, they began to cry and one of the boys told me that the baby died last night. Bridget had gone to the priest about the burial.

The potatoes we stored in the pits last year seemed to melt away before we could eat them, and father had some trouble to keep enough to plant again in April. At first, the crop began to grow as in other years, but this morning we smelt the terrible stench once more. For a moment, no one spoke, and then my father said, "That would be the blight." He said to my mother, "God help us, Mary. I did not think it could happen twice over." Then he went out to the field.

When he came back he said, "I have dug ten ridges today, and this is all I have." He put a small bag of potatoes into my mother's hands. "All the rest are black and stinking."

That night my father went and sat beside the dung heap. I heard him talking, but there was no one out there except the pig. Mother went out to him and asked, "Have you a prayer said, Sean?"

"I have."

"You are a good man, Sean," said my mother. "We must trust in God."

Mother killed one of the fowls today to make a broth. She hopes it will make Annie well but our poor baby looks so thin and lies so still in my arms that I had not the heart to tell her about Bridget's child.

People bring their children to the poorhouse (below) and beg the guardians to let them in, but the place is filled with people, some with the fever on them, and all who come in these times are turned away.

DECEMBER 1846

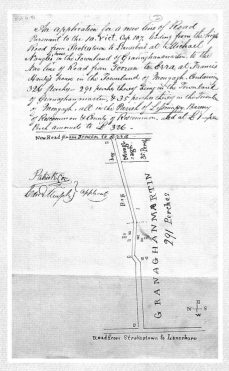

These are bad times, sure enough. The winter grows more terrible every day, and there is nothing left to eat but a few cabbages and turnips from the garden. Father barely has the strength to cut turf, and the pile beside the house grows less and less each day, until it is almost gone. Michael and I made a promise, each to the other, that we would never speak of being hungry, but the little ones clamor for food and we cannot stop them.

Pat Feeney brought his family to the poorhouse, but there was no room for them. But Bridget's prayers were answered, for there is work set on in the neighborhood. It is to split a hill for a new road. People call it the "meal road," for the little money the laborers get is spent to buy the yellow meal, but it is never enough to fill their children's bellies. Pat had not a taste of food for three days before he started, and must walk four miles to the place each day.

Michael and I saw a man lying dead in a ditch and the flesh on him so wasted that at first we thought him to be a bundle of rags. We were told that he was working on the road and had not the strength for the journey home. Now his wife must take his place.

I wonder, will we end in the poorhouse? 'Tis a fearful place. Grandmother said she would rather die than walk through the gates.

When I brought these into the house, Mother said to me, "that will be the last of the vegetables, I can see it from your face."

I said, "What will we do?" but she shook her head and did not speak.

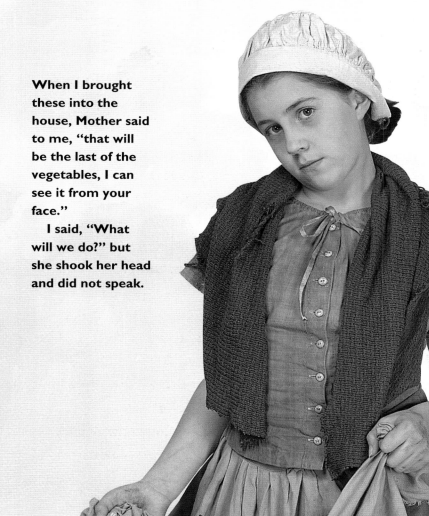

A Letter to the Agent

Father went to our priest, Father Doyle, to write a letter to Mr. Simpson, who is Major Lloyd's agent, for we cannot pay the rent. Father Doyle wrote on the paper that we are starving and have not a potato

to eat. Father brought it to the office, but Mr. Simpson says he will throw us out of the house if the money is not paid. There are many here in the same desperate state, and Mr. Simpson would turn us all off if he could, I am sure.

JANUARY—MARCH 1847

The last of the fowls is eaten, and the pig sold, for we had nothing to feed him. Mother sold her good shawl, but it did not bring much. There is a stock of Indian meal come into the village, and Mother and I went to see if we could buy some. It is queer stuff, being yellow, and indeed, people call it "Peel's brimstone." Who Peel might be, I do not know. I suppose he is an Englishman.

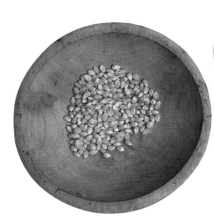

This is the appearance of the yellow meal before it is milled (left) and afterward (above).

Soup Kitchens

A soup kitchen is opened up in a town not five miles from here. Pat and his family went to it, having nothing to eat after the road making was stopped. The soup given is stirabout, made from water, yellow meal and rice, and for the shame of standing in a line for all to see, your bowl will be filled.

At the soup kitchens, the stirabout is boiled in big iron cauldrons that are dug into the ground.

NOTICE.

I HEREBY give Notice to the LABOURERS and POOR HOUSEHOLDERS on LORD CALEDON'S ESTATE, that his LORDSHIP and LADY CALEDON have instructed me to open

THREE SOUP KITCHENS,

In convenient parts of his Lordship's property, to supply Soup and Bread at a very moderate price; and that such will be ready for delivery *at Twelve o'Clock, on Monday, the 28th inst.,* at the following places, viz. :—

The Model Farm;
The Village of Dyan; and at the
House of J. Marshall, at Brantry Wood;

And will be continued every Day, at the same hour, until farther Notice (Sundays excepted).

The Labourers employed at Drainage and other Works, can send their Children to the most convenient of the above places, for a supply of Soup, &c., which shall be sent to them hot in Covered Cans. And in order to encourage useful industry amongst the Children, I hereby offer a Premium of 2d. per Bushel, for Bruised or Pounded Whin Tops, properly prepared as food for Horses and Cows, delivered at any of the above-mentioned places.

LORD CALEDON has desired his CARETAKERS to permit the Children to gather the Whin Tops on any grounds in his Lordship's possession, particularly in the large STOCK FARM of KEDEW, and in the Plantations of DROMORE, DROMESS, and LISMULLYDOWN; and I am sure the Tenantry will also encourage so useful an occupation at the present moment, when it is so desirable to use the strictest economy in the feeding of our Cattle.

HENRY L. PRENTICE,
AGENT.

N.B.—A Double supply of Food will be Cooked on Saturdays.

CALEDON, 19th December, 1846.   ARMAGH:—PRINTED BY J. M'WATTERS.

When we returned, Mother showed the yellow meal to Father. "Look, Sean. What will I do with it?"

She set the meal to boil, and we all ate some. Whether there was something wrong about the cooking, I do not know, but we were all taken with the flux and our bowels turned to water. It is brimstone indeed!

Now the relief work is finished, and the roads are full of beggars who barely stand upright for want of food. This morning I found two children searching our dung heap for cabbage stalks. The boy told me they had left their mother's body by the road, for they could not carry her. His mouth was stained green from eating grass.

Annie died last night, and Mother will not part with her, but sits before the empty fire, saying the rosary and holding our poor baby in her arms.

Ration tickets, like the ones below, are given at the soup kitchen. Men and women get a whole ration, children a half. Those without a ticket will have nothing to eat.

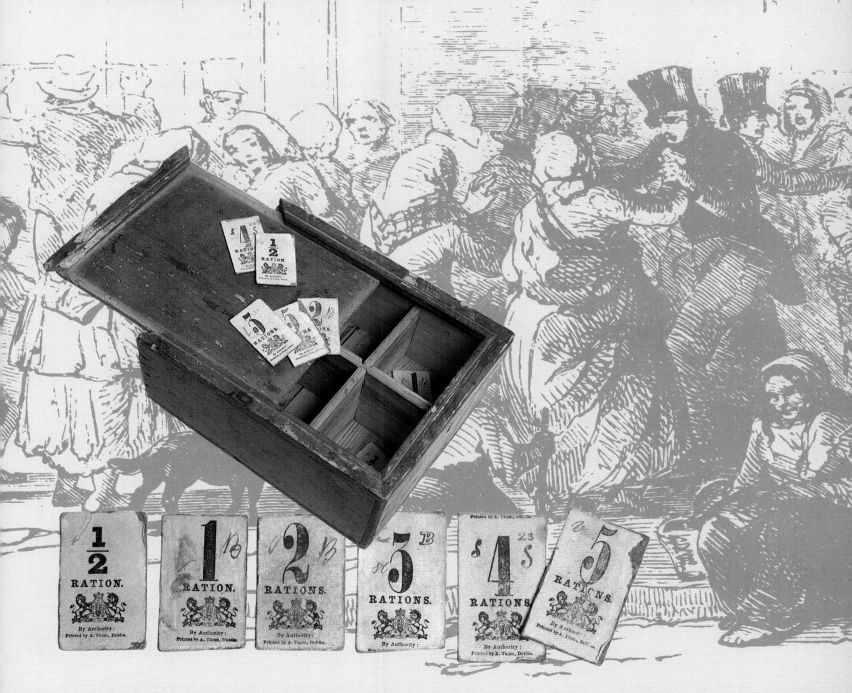

APRIL 1847

Grandmother died in the night, God rest her soul. Her body was swelled from hunger. This morning I went to bring the priest, but was told that Father Doyle had the black fever on him. So many have the fever in the village that the dying bear the dead upon their backs to the burial ground and leave them there. On my return I passed Pat's cabin. The door was shut, and when I opened it, I saw all the family lying dead within — the four children huddled together upon one bed and Pat on the other. Bridget lay beside him, on the floor. The poor creature must have dragged herself to fasten the door when all hope was gone. Michael took blood from one of Major Lloyd's cows tonight. He cut the beast's skin, drew off a quart of blood and brought it home in a bowl. Mother baked it into a cake. I

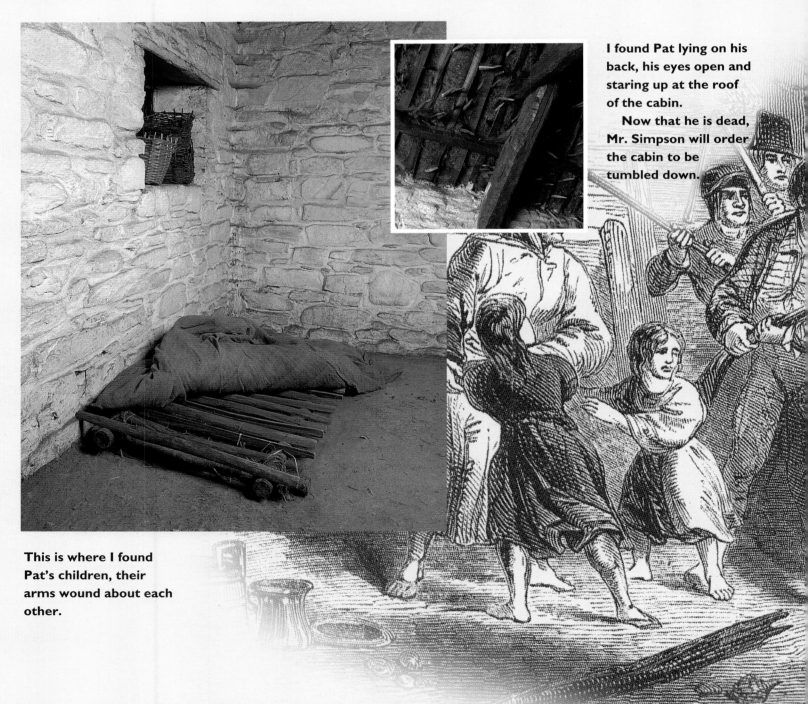

I found Pat lying on his back, his eyes open and staring up at the roof of the cabin.

Now that he is dead, Mr. Simpson will order the cabin to be tumbled down.

This is where I found Pat's children, their arms wound about each other.

was glad of it, for we had had nothing but nettle soup for five days, there being nothing to be had at the soup kitchen. But it is a dangerous thing that Michael has done; one of Mr. Simpson's men shot a boy last week and killed him, for stealing turnips. The family had eaten the dog the day before. Others have eaten bad roots and berries, not knowing them to be poisonous, and died from it.

Notice to Quit

It is Mr. Simpson's plan to turn as many off the land as he can, for Major Lloyd wants the grass for cows. We have heard that he has run into debt because of the money owing for rent, but he cannot be starving as we are. Mr. Simpson brought three of our neighbors notices to quit, and said if they did not leave their houses, he would cause them to be thrown down around their heads. The families tried to stop the landlord's men getting into their houses, but it was no use.

I said a prayer for Pat and his family. Mother said, "Poor Pat, now his trouble is over," and I wondered if we too must leave this world before our troubles can be over.

MAY 1847

Our neighbor, Mr. O'Mahoney, was turned off his land yesterday. The O'Mahoneys' house is not half a mile away from ours. When we heard the noise we went to see what the matter was, and found poor Mr. O'Mahoney on his knees before Major Lloyd's men, begging them not to destroy his home. The men paid him no heed, but pushed him

Major Lloyd has offered some of the tenants money if they will leave their homes. To others, like the O'Mahoneys, who owe too much rent, he offers nothing.

I do not understand how any Christian man can take a bar such as this and tumble down a house, being sure — as he must be — that the man and his family will afterwards die from sickness and want.

aside, and when he tried to follow them, the leader turned and beat him so that he fell to the ground. It was terrible to see him try to rise to his feet while Mrs. O'Mahoney wept and the children wailed.

Father stepped forward to help Mr. O'Mahoney, but the men shouted at him to stay back and began to tear the roof off. Some of them pushed the ends of their crowbars between the stones of the walls, so that they started to fall, and soon there was little left of the house but tumbled walls.

After the wreckers had gone, we helped the O'Mahoneys to make a scalpeen, or shelter, of their ruined house, where they could spend the night. This morning, they must ask to be let into the poorhouse. There is nowhere else for them to go.

Last night, I looked through the door at the bedroom where I sleep with my brothers and sisters, and saw Annie's cradle, empty now. I wonder how long Major Lloyd will let us stay in this house, and what will become of us.

JUNE 1847

Mr. Simpson has written down a list of tenants who are going to America. He told Father that a new law has been made in England, and Major Lloyd has to support us, his tenants, or pay for our passage to America. It costs less money to send us to America than to keep us here in the poorhouse.

Mr. Simpson told us that Major Lloyd has offered us money for a passage to America, to be rid of us. Mother thinks Margaret will not last the winter, and Father has no hope of a potato crop next year, there being nothing to plant. Everyone has heard tales of those who have fared well in the New World. Whether they are true I do not know, but whatever it is like in America, surely it must be a better place than this. Certainly, it must be better than the poorhouse; all who pass through those gates die of the fever. We have heard that the corpses are thrown into pits without a priest or a prayer, there being no coffins.

We have a passage on a ship secured, and all that remains is to make bundles of the blankets, pots and pans, and such clothes as we have left, and to use our small stock

I went out by myself and took scraps of heather and gorse to bring with me. I cannot imagine a land without these, but perhaps they do not grow in America.

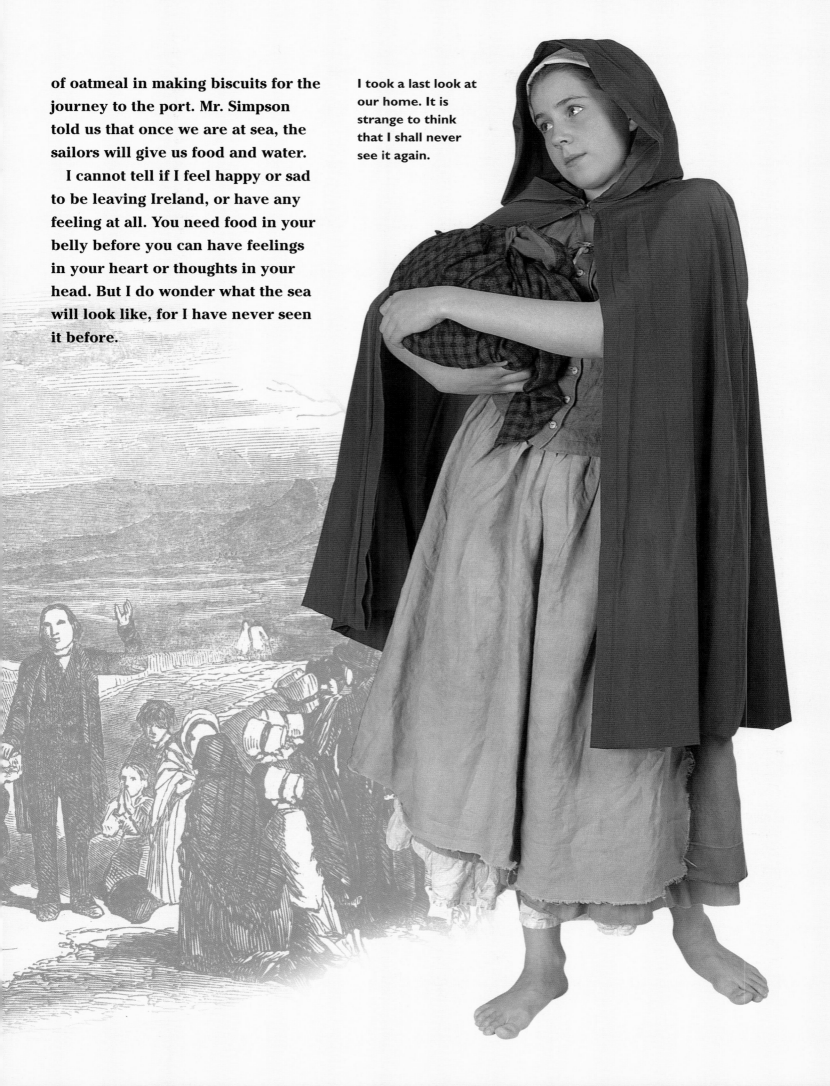

of oatmeal in making biscuits for the journey to the port. Mr. Simpson told us that once we are at sea, the sailors will give us food and water.

I cannot tell if I feel happy or sad to be leaving Ireland, or have any feeling at all. You need food in your belly before you can have feelings in your heart or thoughts in your head. But I do wonder what the sea will look like, for I have never seen it before.

I took a last look at our home. It is strange to think that I shall never see it again.

JULY 1847

We are not often allowed on the deck, which is full of ropes, barrels, sacks, and other things to trip over and send yourself sprawling.

This (inset) is the top of the hatch. Most of the time we must stay below, in the hold, where there is little light, and no fresh air.

We were taken to the port in a cart — four days' journey. I have never seen so many people in one place as there were on that quayside. I was more than once knocked over in the jostling and bustling before we were taken out to the ship on a rowing boat, and pulled on board like so many bundles. A man laid hold of my legs to pull me down on the deck, and then dragged Michael down on top of me!

The sea is beautiful, although I do not like the way the boat moves from side to side. We stood on the deck to get a last look at Ireland. I wonder, shall I ever see it again? Michael says he never wants to see it again, and will learn to speak English as quick as he can, for the Irish is just bad luck.

I don't know how we will manage, for we have not been given half the

food we were promised, and with the water being so foul and muddy that it might have been drawn from a ditch. There are hearths on deck, where you may cook, and in the evening we made our first meal on board ship. No sooner had we taken the pot from the fire, when there was a shout from above our heads and a boy who was standing in the ropes, or rigging as the sailors call it, poured a great jug of water over

PASSENGERS CONTRACT TICKET

SHP. No. ⚓ 147

Ship of tons register burthen
to sail from on the

_____ day of _____ 18__

NAMES

I engage that the Parties herein named shall be provided with a Steerage Passage to the Port of in the United States of America, in the Ship with not less than Ten Cubic Feet for Luggage for each adult, for the sum of £ - - in payment.

In addition to any Provisions which the Passengers may themselves bring, Water and Provisions will be supplied to each Passenger by the Master of the Ship, as required by Law and also Fires and suitable places for cooking.

Signed by

On behalf of State Printers at the ULSTER AMERICAN FOLK PARK

The ticket — our last hope. Morning and night, I pray to God and His Holy Mother to keep us safe and, in between, try to forget the stories I have heard about shipwrecks.

it. One of the rules of the ship is that the fire must be put out at nightfall, and a soaking will be in it for you, too, if you are standing beside it.

AUGUST 1847

In fine weather, Michael and I like to stand at the bottom of the ladder and look through the hatch at the blue sky and white clouds above us. At first, we talked a good deal about the food we ate before the bad times. Michael was remembering Mother's stirabout, oatmeal thick with buttermilk and fresh butter melted into it, when I suddenly felt my belly turn over. It was the sea sickness. There is not one person here who has not suffered from it, and the hold is so thick with the smell of it that you can scarcely draw your breath. The hold is a treacherous place to live. Whenever there is a bad storm, half the bunks crash down on the floor, sending us with them, and then it is desperate trouble to put them back up again, especially when the floor is ankle-deep in water and other things (which I shall not name).

It is very crowded down here in the hold. We have been granted a single bunk — Mother, Father, Michael, Patrick, Margaret, Seamus and myself — and very cramped we find ourselves, although it is not so bad as being berthed with strangers.

Fever has broken out in the hold, and many of the passengers — my sister Margaret amongst them — have the sickness on them so fierce that we think they must die of it. All the time, they cry out, "Water, for God's sake, water!" One man, chosen by the other passengers, went to the captain with a can to show him the bad state of it, but the captain only answered that he could not help us for there was nothing else to be had.

What a torment to be surrounded by water, with nothing to drink!

*　　*　　*

My poor sister Margaret died yesterday, God rest her soul. Some of the sailors wrapped her in a meal sack with a weight tied into it, and cast her over the side of the ship with the others who had died. The family said a rosary and Father said a prayer for her, there being no priest on the ship.

You never saw so many people as rushed on deck, hoping for a sight of America.

SEPTEMBER 1847

I have made a friend. Her name is Sinead Costello, and she is sailing with her mother. Her father died in an accident at the road works, and her uncle, who is already in New York, offered to pay their passage to America. He is going to meet them and help Sinead to find a job as a maid.

We were standing in my favorite place on the ship, looking up at the sky and listening to the sailors singing on deck as they worked, when we heard someone shout out, "land, land!" We both shouted, "America!" and then I ran to our bunk to tell Mother. "Why wouldn't it be," said she, "after seven weeks in this hole that isn't fit to keep a rat in?" but she was smiling when she said it. It is the first time I have seen her smile since Margaret died.

We could see the land for two days before the ship put in to port, green hills and farms, but at the quayside there were rows of big houses, some as tall as four stories. I heard one man say there are grander houses in Dublin, but as I have never been there, I cannot tell you if that is true. But sure there cannot be so many houses in Dublin as there are here, nor so many people, for there were four ships from Ireland put in today besides our own.

* * *

When we left the ship, it felt strange to be standing upon land again, but I had little time to enjoy the feeling as we were herded off, like so many cows, for the doctor to examine us.

I was afraid that the doctor would find the fever on us and turn us back, but he didn't. Instead, his clerk tied a paper label on to our clothes, just as if we were parcels, and then we were rushed along in a great press of people, out into the street. I feared to be separated from my family and my bundle in the crush, for there were plenty ready to tug it away from me if I gave them any chance. But I held fast to my few belongings until I found myself safe again with Mother and Father.

In the last days of our journey on the ship, Mother helped a woman called Mrs. O'Rourke, whose baby was sick with the fever. Mother thought he might live to see the new world, but as we came in sight of the harbor, we heard Mrs. O'Rourke cry out. The child had died in her arms.

OCTOBER 1847

Shall I tell you how the O'Flynn family fared in their new home? Well, you can be sure we learned English as fast as we could, although it took Mother a long time, she not going about in the world as we did.

Finding work was hard, as many would not hire Irish people. They even wrote in the newspaper, "No Irish Need Apply." Sinead's uncle said, "If it's work you're after, you'll be losing that O' in O'Flynn. It's a rare Yankee will give a job to an Irishman."

My brother Michael said, "Sure, won't they know we're Irish as soon as we open our mouths?"

Father gave out to him, "If we wanted to put food in those mouths, we would listen to the man." Then he smiled at us and said, "We should have a new name for the new world. So Flynn it is."

Some people call Ireland "the old country." It makes me think of an old house where no one wants to live anymore. Mother tells us not to speak of it at all. 'Tis a land full of graves, she says.

New York

I shall never forget that first night in New York — Sinead's uncle came to meet herself and Mrs. Costello from the ship, and kindly showed us to a lodging house. It was dark when he brought us there, and I ran round a corner and straight into a great bellowing thing that crashed into my legs and almost threw me to the ground. I gave a scream, thinking it must be one of the robbers Sinead's uncle had warned us against, but when I looked down, I saw it was a pig!

When I looked out of the window in the morning, I saw half a dozen pigs in the street, and dogs as well, all pushing their snouts into such heaps of rubbish as I never saw before. New York is dirty, sure enough, but the shops! I could have spent the rest of my life looking through the windows at the wonderful things, but it's work we have to find.

Father and Michael got hired to mend roads, and I found a job as a maid in a big house. You may be sure that I worked twice as hard as did the Yankee girls, so that the mistress would not think me lazy or dirty on account of being Irish!

When we arrived at the lodging house, I untied my bundle and laid on the bed the piece of turf and the heather and gorse I'd picked back home. They looked very small and squashed. Ireland seems very far away — and it is, for I heard a man say we had traveled over 3,000 miles.

Father saved my wages for a pair of boots. They are the finest I have ever had.

AFTERWORD 1884

All that was long ago. It was hard at first in a new country but I did well enough. In 1854 I was married to Paddy Byrne, who came from Ireland in black '47, as I did. We have five children grown. They know no bit of the Irish, being true Americans, born and raised here in New York. My brother Michael married a lovely girl, and has eight fine children to his name. Patrick and Seamus went out West, and we know little of them.

Michael and I do not often speak of the bad times — indeed, I believe we have talked of it but once these past twenty years, but you can be sure that we do not forget our home in Ireland, or my grandmother, or baby Annie, or poor sister Margaret, God rest them.

I still have my bits of heather and gorse, and a few crumbs of turf. Sometimes I bring them out when nobody is looking, and touch them, and think of the old country, the grass and rocks and the tumbled cottages and the graves of the poor ones who died starving. It makes me sad to look at them, but then another feeling comes over me. Happiness. Because, thank God, I survived. Because I am glad to be alive.

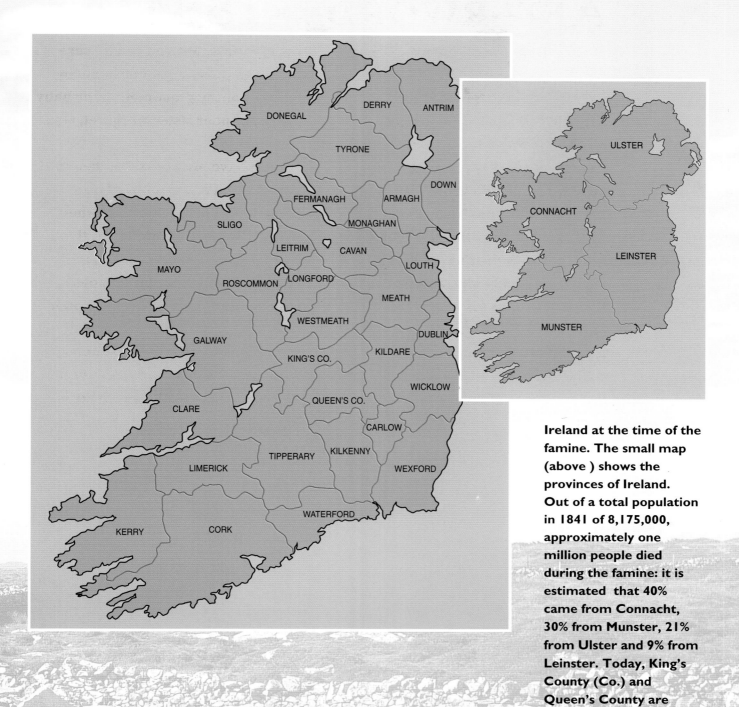

Ireland at the time of the famine. The small map (above) shows the provinces of Ireland. Out of a total population in 1841 of 8,175,000, approximately one million people died during the famine: it is estimated that 40% came from Connacht, 30% from Munster, 21% from Ulster and 9% from Leinster. Today, King's County (Co.) and Queen's County are named Offaly and Laois.

GLOSSARY

Black fever typhus, an infectious fever that has since died out in the developed world. An eruption of purple spots all over the body was followed by prostration, delirium, and then death.

Boxty potato pancakes

Brimstone an old-fashioned term for sulfur, a natural element whose yellow powder burns with a blue flame and stifling smell. Believed at the time of Mary's journal to fuel the fires of hell.

Flux diarrhea

Laissez faire political policy of non-interference

Loy plough-like utensil used in planting potatoes

New World America (Europe being the Old World)

Noggin large wooden cup for measuring liquid

Peel Sir Robert Peel, British Prime Minister 1834–45, 1841–46

Poorhouse state-provided refuge for the destitute, where food and shelter was given in return for work

Relief work created by the government for the famine victims

Rosary series of prayers said by Roman Catholics and counted on a string of beads, itself also referred to as a rosary.

Scalpeen a shelter

Slane utensil for cutting turf

Spud potato

Stirabout porridge made with oatmeal and buttermilk

Turf peat, dug and dried for fuel

INDEX

PLACES TO VISIT

The Ulster American Folk Park
Castleton, Omagh, County Tyrone BT78 5QY, Northern Ireland.
Website: www.folkpark.com

The folk park tells the story of the thousands of emigrants who left Ireland for America in the 18th and 19th centuries. The museum has 23 buildings, including restored originals, on an outdoor site. Costumed guides use "living history" to bring the past to life, as it was both on land and on board ship.
  The park also houses the Centre for Migration Studies, which offers excellent research facilities, including a computerized database.

The Famine Museum
Strokestown Park, County Roscommon, Ireland
Website: www.strokestownpark.ie/intro.himl

Strokestown Park House was the family seat of the Pakenham Mahon family from 1653 until 1981. Spanning almost 350 years of Irish history, it is a unique resource which is now widely regarded as the single best example, in Ireland, of a privately funded restoration project. The stables have been converted to house the Famine Museum which, as well as providing an interpretation of the house and its history, explores the issues of famine and emigration in a wider historical context.

BIBLIOGRAPHY

Coleman, Terry. *Passage to America.* London: Pimlico, 1972.

Hobhouse, Henry. *Seeds of Change: Six Plants That Transformed Mankind.* London: Papermac, 1985.

Keegan, Gerald. *Famine Diary: Journey to a New World,* ed. James J. Mangan. Dublin: Wolfhound Press, 1991.

Killen, John, ed. *The Famine Decade: Contemporary Accounts 1841–51.* Belfast: Blackstaff Press, 1995.

Laxton, Edward. *The Famine Ships: The Irish Exodus to America 1846–51.* London: Bloomsbury, 1996.

Litton, Helen. *The Irish Famine: An Illustrated History.* Dublin: Wolfhound Press, 1994.

Nicholson, Asenath. *Annals of the Famine in Ireland, ed.* Maureen Murphy. Dublin: The Lilliput Press, 1998.

Poirteir, Cathal. *Famine Echoes.* Dublin: Gill & Macmillan, 1995.

Woodham Smith, Cecil. *The Great Hunger: Ireland 1845–9.* London: Hamish Hamilton, 1962.